WOODS ETC.

Woods etc.   ALICE OSWALD

faber and faber

First published in 2005
by Faber and Faber Limited
3 Queen Square London WC1N 3AU

Photoset by RefineCatch Ltd, Bungay, Suffolk
Printed in England by T. J. International Ltd, Padstow, Cornwall

A CIP record for this book
is available from the British Library

ISBN 0-571-21852-0

10 9 8 7 6 5 4 3 2 1

Contents

WOODS ETC.

Sea Poem

what is water in the eyes of water
loose inquisitive fragile anxious
a wave, a winged form
splitting up into sharp glances

what is the sound of water
after the rain stops you can hear the sea
washing rid of the world's increasing complexity,
making it perfect again out of perfect sand

oscillation endlessly shaken
into an entirely new structure
what is the depth of water
from which time has been rooted out

the depth is the strength of water
it can break glass or sink steel
treading drowners inwards down
what does it taste of

water deep in its own world
steep shafts warm streams
coal salt cod weed
dispersed outflows and flytipping

and the sun and its reflexion
throwing two shadows
what is the beauty of water
sky is its beauty

Seabird's Blessing

We are crowds of seabirds,
makers of many angles,
workers that unpick a web
of the air's threads and tangles.

Pray for us when we fight
the wind one to one;
let not that shuddering strength
smash the cross of the wing-bone.

O God the featherer,
lift us if we fall;
preserve the frenzy in our mouths,
the yellow star in the eyeball.

Christ, make smooth the way
of a creature like a spirit
up from its perverse body
without weight or limit.

Holy ghost of heaven,
blow us clear of the world,
give us the utmost of the air
to heave on and to hold.

Pray for us this weird
bare place – we are screaming
O sky count us not as nothing
O sea count us not as nothing

Birdsong for Two Voices

A spiral ascending the morning,
climbing by means of a song into the sun,
to be sung reciprocally by two birds at intervals
in the same tree but not quite in time.

A song that assembles the earth
out of nine notes and silence.
out of the unformed gloom before dawn
where every tree is a problem to be solved by birdsong.

Crex Crex Corcorovado,
letting the pieces fall where they may,
every dawn divides into the distinct
misgiving between alternate voices

sung repeatedly by two birds at intervals
out of nine notes and silence.
while the sun, with its fingers to the earth,
as the sun proceeds so it gathers instruments:

it gathers the yard with its echoes and scaffolding sounds,
it gathers the swerving away sound of the road,
it gathers the river shivering in a wet field,
it gathers the three small bones in the dark of the eardrum;

it gathers the big bass silence of clouds
and the mind whispering in its shell
and all trees, with their ears to the air,
seeking a steady state and singing it over till it settles.

Owl

last night at the joint of dawn,
an owl's call opened the darkness

miles away, more than a world beyond this room

and immediately, I was in the woods again,
poised, seeing my eyes seen,
hearing my listening heard

under a huge tree improvised by fear

dead brush falling then a star
straight through to God
founded and fixed the wood

then out, until it touched the town's lights,
an owl's elsewhere swelled and questioned

twice, like you might lean and strike
two matches in the wind

Woods etc.

footfall, which is a means so steady
and in small sections wanders through the mind
unnoticed, because it beats constantly,
sweeping together the loose tacks of sound

I remember walking once into increasing
woods, my hearing like a widening wound.
first your voice and then the rustling ceasing.
the last glow of rain dead in the ground

that my feet kept time with the sun's imaginary
changing position, hoping it would rise
suddenly from scattered parts of my body
into the upturned apses of my eyes.

no clearing in that quiet, no change at all.
in my throat the little mercury line
that regulates my speech began to fall
rapidly the endless length of my spine

Leaf

for J.O. and L.O.

the leaf that now lies being made
in its shell of scale, the hush of things
unseen inside, the heartbeat of dead wood.
the slow through-flow that feeds
a form curled under, hour by hour
the thick reissuing starlike shapes
of cells and pores and water-rods
which builds up, which becomes a pressure,
a gradual fleshing out of a longing for light,
a small hand unfolding, feeling about.
into that hand the entire
object of the self being coldly placed,
the provisional, the inexplicable I
in mid-air, meeting the wind and dancing

Wood Not Yet Out

closed and containing everything, the land
leaning all round to block it from the wind,
a squirrel sprinting in startles and sees
sections of distance tilted through the trees
and where you jump the fence a flap of sacking
does for a stile, you walk through webs, the cracking
bushtwigs break their secrecies, the sun
vanishes up, instantly come and gone.
once in, you hardly notice as you move,
the wood keeps lifting up its hope, I love
to stand among the last trees listening down
to the releasing branches where I've been –
the rain, thinking I've gone, crackles the air
and calls by name the leaves that aren't yet there

A Winged Seed

I was born bewildered
at dawn when the rain ends;

uniquely no one in particular, a pauper in a shack of flower.

At dawn, when the rain ends,
things drift about seeking shape.

I saw pollen pass through trees
in no rush
possessing nothing, not even weight.

I set out, taking my whole world with me,
wrapping myself round in my own identity as thin as a soap-film,

and all that day I was a wind-born eye.
I couldn't put myself
at rest, not even for one second.

Increasingly unfocused, spinning
through the disintegrating kingdom of a garden,
and going nowhere
and feeling myself at all angles,

I was huge,
like you might sow a seed guitar,
a cryptic shape of spheres and wires.

Sisyphus

This man Sisyphus, he has to push
his dense unthinkable rock
through bogs woods crops glittering
optical rivers and hoof-sucked holes,
as high as starlight as low as granite,
and every inch of it he feels
the vertical stress of the sky
draw trees narrow, wear water round
and the lithe, cold-blooded grasses
weighed so down they have to hang their tips like cats' tails;
and it rains it blows but the mad delicate world
will not let will not let him out
and when he prays, he hears God passing with a
swish at this, a knock at that.

There is not a soft or feeling part,
the rock's heart is only another bone;
now he knows he will not get back home,
his whole outlook is a black rock;
like a foetus, undistractedly listening
to the clashing and whistling and tapping of another world,
he has to endure his object,
he has to oppose his patience to his perceptions . . .
and there is neither mouth
nor eye, there is not anything
so closed, so abstract as this rock
except innumerable other rocks
that lie down under the shady trees
or chafe slowly in the seas.

The secret is to walk evading nothing
through rain sleet darkness wind,
not to abandon the spirit of repetition:
there are the green and yellow trees, the dog,
the dark barrier of water,
there goes the thundercloud shaking its blue wolf's head;
and the real effort is to stare
unreconciled at how the same things are,
but he is half aware he is
lost or at any rate straining
out of the earth into a lifted sphere
(dust in his hair, a dark blood thread from his ear)
and jumps at shapes, like on a country road,
in heavy boots, heading uphill in silence.

Once his wide-armed shadow
came at him kicking,
his monkey counterpart pinioned to the rock;
the two grappled and the rock
stopped dead, pushed between them in suspension
and it was fear, quivering motion
holding them there, like in the centre of a flower
the small anxiety that sets it open
and for an hour, all he could think was
caught in a state of shadow – this persistent
breathing pushing sound, this fear of falling,
fear of lucidity, of flight, of something
bending towards him, but he pushed he pushed
until the sun sank and the shadow slunk away.

'I woke early when the grass was still a standing choir,
each green flower lifting a drop of water –
an hour of everything flashing out of darkness,
whole trees with their bones,

whole rivers with their kicks and throws,
there I walked lifting a drop of water;
I came to this cold field, the crowded
smoky-headed grasses singing of patience:
'Oh what does it matter?' they sang,
'longer and longer and all day
on one foot is the practice of grasses'
which raised in me a terrible cry of hope
and there I stood, waiting for the sun
to draw the water from my head . . .'

But Sisyphus is confused; he has to think
one pain at a time, like an insect
imprisoned in a drop of water;
he tries again, he distorts his body to the task
and a back-pain passes slowly
low down in the spine – a fine red thread
that winds his hands and feet in the struggle of movement;
and Sisyphus is a hump, Sisyphus is a stone
somewhere far away, feeling the sun
flitter to and fro with closed eyes,
unable to loiter, an unborn creature
seeking a womb, saying Sisyphus Sisyphus . . .
and he stares forward but there's nothing there
and backward but he can't perceive it.

Song of a Stone

there was a woman from the north
picked a stone up from the earth.
when the stone began to dream
it was a flower folded in

when the flower began to fruit
it was a circle full of light,
when the light began to break
it was a flood across a plain

when the plain began to stretch
the length scattered from the width
and when the width began to climb
it was a lark above a cliff

the lark singing for its life
was the muscle of a heart,
the heart flickering away
was an offthrow of the sea

and when the sea began to dance
it was the labyrinth of a conscience,
when the conscience pricked the heart
it was a man lost in thought

like milk that sours in the light,
like vapour twisting in the heat,
the thought was fugitive – a flare of gold –
it was an iris in a field

and when the man began to murmur
it was a question with no answer,
when the question changed its form
it was the same point driven home

it was a problem, a lamentation:
'What the buggery's going on?
This existence is an outrage!
Give me an arguer to shout with!'

and when the arguer appeared
it was an angel of the Lord,
and when the angel touched his chest,
it was his heartbeat being pushed

and when his heart began to break
it was the jarring of an earthquake
when the earth began to groan
they laid him in it six by one

dark bigger than his head,
pain swifter than his blood,
as good as gone, what could he do?
as deep as stone, what could he know?

Autobiography of a Stone

on this air-borne earth where the one thrust of things is endlessly
     upward,
I, Stone, fell into affliction,
worse than
the annealing of glass through the whole series of endurable pains

and worse.
and that was when I, Stone, became
this final measure
of drawing my whole body inward into my skull.

I became Excluded Stone, Stone-in-hiding.
who lies not peering out
in a fold of the winds and
hearing myself being shouted for   oh

if the wind were a voice I could contend with . . .
but I am moving only very slowly,
lasting out earth and
keeping my gift under darkness.

The Stone Skimmer

Going down through the two small fields,
disturbing the small-seeing flies   he brushes
the restless thistles, their dried skins hooked to their bones.
brimming flowering dimming diminishing.
Among the thistles and the whisking pools of the wind
he's walking   he can almost feel
the spent fur of his flesh, a seed-ghost on a gust
condemned to float in endless widening circles.

Eyeless stones, their silence swells and breathes easily in water,
barely move in the wombs of rivers.
His mind so rushed and slovenly, full of forms
brimming flowering dimming diminishing:
into the five inch space between heaven and heaven
he's skimming a stone   it's just the smack of it
contacting water, the amazing length
of light keeps lifting up his slid-down strength

Danaides

intermittently they stop
with plybone spines
and fingers rusted
open and hearing
their work pouring
through these holes
their minds swinging
side to side
and far away
their feet hollowed
out and gone
smooth with turning
they stare down
in horrible fag-break
gloom at water's
cloning loops its
frays and flumes
and vacillations and
clings and rips
and cloops and
splashy cleats all
water's wilful unresistance
to its own
cascading condition and
one by one
begin to lift
to lift it
like a child

(The Danaides murdered their husbands. When they died they had to carry water
in a leaking jar as a punishment.)

Lovesong for Three Children

It starts at pitch quiet
when sleep cloths up sound
and the dead tongue keeps
jointing and disjointing words,

when breathing blows the ear's
doors a little open and
my heart in note form
steals from its instrument   O

now it begins to sing
O those three children and
sings it until the light
infiltrates this cone of bones

and I can see you,
my voice, hanging in the
belfry-emptiness of the throat,
your two ropes swinging slightly.

Walking past a Rose this June Morning

is my heart a rose?   how unspeakable
is my heart a rose?   how unspeakable
is my heart folded to dismantle?   how unspeakable
is a rose folded in its nerves?   how unspeakable
is my heart secretly overhanging us?   pause
is there a new world   known only to breathing?
now inhale what I remember.   pause.   how unbreathable

this is my heart out.   how unspeakable
this is my risen skin.   how unthinkable
this is my tense touch-sensitive heart
this is its mass made springy by the rain
this loosening compression of hope.   how unworkable
is an invisible ray lighting up your lungs?   how invisible?
is it a weightless rapture?   pause.   how weightless?

now trace a breath-map in the air.   how invisible?
is a rose a turning cylinder of senses?   how unspeakable
is this the ghost of the heart, the actual
the inmost deceleration of its thought?   how unspeakable
is everything still speeding around us?   pause
is my heart the centre?   how unbearable
is the rain a halo?   how unbearable

Sonnet

towards winter flowers, forms of ecstatic water,
    chalk lies dry with all its throats open.
winter flowers last maybe one frost
    chalk drifts its heap through billions of slow sea-years;
    rains and pools and opens its wombs,
    bows its back, shows its bone.
  both closing towards each other
  at the dead end of the year – one
  woken through, the others thrown into flower,
holding their wings at the ready in an increasing state of crisis.
    burrowed into and crumbled, carrying
these small supernumerary powers founded on breath:
  chalk with all its pits and pores,
winter flowers, smelling of a sudden entering elsewhere.

Head of a Dandelion

This is the dandelion with its thousand faculties

like an old woman taken by the neck
and shaken to pieces.

This is the dust-flower flitting away.

This is the flower of amnesia.
It has opened its head to the wind,
all havoc and weakness,

as if a wooden man should stroll through fire . . .

In this unequal trial, one thing
controls the invisible violence of the air,

the other gets smashed and will not give in.

One thing flexes its tail causing widespread devastation,
it takes hold of the trees, it blows their failings out of them,
it throws in sideways, it flashes the river upriver;

the other thing gives up its skin and bones,
goes up in smoke, lets go of its ashes . . .

and this is the flower of no property,
this is the wind-bitten dandelion
worn away to its one recalcitrant element

like when Osiris
blows his scales and weighs the soul with a feather.

For Many Hours there's been an Old Couple
Standing at that Window

Awake so long, with only dark to feed on,
long ago they remember walking very slowly to the window.
They let their hearts sink to one side
and stood in their old clothes, growing frost at the edges.

For hours, nothing else was there,
only their eyes increasing into tiny stars. And then
Sunrise –
a sudden eruption of circumstances.

This had never happened before.
There had never been so much beauty.
The sky, up to now unknown,
burned a way out through a nearby horizon.
Their eyes were in disarray.

They began to sway, rubbing their hands together,
they moved cautiously to the brink of one glance and back.

And at each turn, morning was more there,
like in the winter's splitting cold a crocus
opens and then more opens.

They saw the horizon growing hard and contracted
as a steel template dipped in water
and they leaned, it looked as if their wings were caught in their
    coats.

All up the fields there was whispering and singing
and a whole surrounding atmosphere of persuasion:
Please realise, friends, Time is moving in this neighbourhood.
This is Dawn, the unspeakable iridescence of all swiftness,
impatiently brushing past, be quick . . .

But their eyesight slid down,
it fell at their feet, they
shrank into sleep, their mouths
dried, their dreams rattled in their pods.

After all, they have only their accustomed answers.
They hardly know who they are, they feel like twists
of jointed grass, going on growing and growing.

Field

Easternight, the mind's midwinter

I stood in the big field behind the house
at the centre of all visible darkness

a brick of earth, a block of sky,
there lay the world, wedged
between its premise and its conclusion

some star let go a small sound on a thread.

almost midnight – I could feel the earth's
soaking darkness squeeze and fill its darkness,
everything spinning into the spasm of midnight

and for a moment, this high field unhorizoned
hung upon nothing, barking for its owner

burial, widowed, moonless, seeping

docks, grasses, small windflowers, weepholes, wires

Ideogram for Green

In the invisible places
Where the first leaves start

    Green breathes growth

Simultaneously dreaming into position what impinges on its
    edges
So that grasses of different kinds should appear in the world

    Green hides roots, lights flowers

    Green shines rain
Like a looked at thing being turned in all directions

A rising slope seen intermittently through a wood,
    The wind tunes green by moving its shadows,
    The hedge-cutter slashes it down,

    Green slows tools, chokes outlets

Like something struggling to be held
And underfoot and in the heart and

Keeping that promise upon which the sunlight takes its bearings

Like through each leaf light is being somehow
Put together in a rush and wedged in a narrow place

Marginalia at the Edge of the Evening

now the sound of the trees is worldwide

and I'm still here/not here
at the very lifting edge of evening.

and I should be up there. Bathing children.

because it's late, the bike's asleep on its feet,
the fields hang to the sun by slackened lines

and when the wind blows it shows
the evening's underside
(when the sun sinks it takes
a moment smaller than a spider)

I saw the luminous underneath of a moth

I saw a blackbird
mouth to the glow of the hour in hieroglyphics . . .

who left the light on the clouds?

pause

the man at the wheel signs his speed on the ringroad.

right here in my reach, time is as thick as stone
and as thin as a flying strand

it's night and somebody's
pushing his mower home

       to the moon

Solomon Grundy

Born on Monday and a tiny
world-containing grain of light
passed through each eye like heaven through a needle.

And on Tuesday
he screamed for a small ear in which to hide.

He rolled on Wednesday, rolled his whole body
full of immense salt spaces, slowly
from one horizon to the other.

And on Thursday, trembling, crippled,
broke beyond his given strength and crawled.

And on Friday he stood upright.

And on Saturday he tested a footstep
and the sky came down and alit on his shoulder
full of various languages in which one bird doesn't answer to
    another.

And on Sunday he dreamed he was flying
and his mind grew gold watching the moon
and he began to sing to the brink of speaking

Poem for Carrying a Baby out of Hospital

like glass, concealed but not lost in light,
has structured into it a stress
that will burst out
suddenly in a shock of cracks, it's all
a matter of terror to hold right
what has a will to fall
and water for instance has the same weakness

the way the level ends of stockstill water break
at the touch of a raindrip, it demands
that kind of calm to walk
with a wafer of glass which if you slip could sheer
straight through a foot or neck
o infinite fear
entirely occupied upon two hands

and even a cobalt blue ingot of glass,
if you think of it, purpose-built
to be melted away, its mass
has an effect which makes it light
it moves through light to the heart of emptiness
though a slight
tap on its surface opens its integral fault

Story of a Man

last time a man was sealed in skin
like an inspoken word sealed in
it was mid-spring, most people arm in arm, most trees whispering
and he could just make out the fluttering light

it was warm, it was days you walk out without a coat
and little rain showers dash across the carpark
and he stood there, like a man on film, going on with his
    heartwork
at last at last he could think clearly

this is myself, he said,
rubbing round all four sides of my breeze-block patience
this is one or two flying strands of my eyes
this is my heart's halo's prismatic subdivisions

there were people bringing chairs to the fire-escapes, peering
    down.
it was mid-spring
and all day, all he could breathe
was the crow's-foot tracks of his sighs' small hollows in the air

then in the half light, it half thawed,
he half, with a mist-hand, waved.
alive in his skin-ruins.
at last at last he could think clearly

Shamrock Café

Last night I thought I'd stop
at the Shamrock café, behind the shop.

It was dead quiet, only me,
my serviette and my cup of tea,

and I was looking at buying one
of the prints on the walls of Neanderthal Man

when I heard this tremulous moaning, just
what a gale beginning or a gust

of a hurricane would make at sea.
I threw an anxious glance at my tea.

There to my horror, was a small
row-boat sinking in a whorl,

and round about the rim a foam
of tea waves crashing in the gloom,

which I drank. All unawares,
a fat girl came to the foot of the stairs

and stood there, with one hand
on the banister, swinging around.

Five Fables of a Length of Flesh

I was once a man. Very tired.
Very gone-inwards glaring outwards at the road.
His pusky eyes, his threadbare hair,
feet frozen in his boots, back sore.

A mouldering man, a powdered and reconstituted
    one
walking the same so on and so on.
Rutty road. Winter etc.
Poached fields, all zugs and water.

I was dying to ditch his head,
maybe put his socks on a twig and stop
caring, just lie there staring up.
I would sing then I would sing if I could

work the words out through this opening,
so done in I was from carrying everything
lungs bones hands belonging to this man
and superintending the rise and fall of breathing.

But as it was, all night he wouldn't let
death help him out or lift me off his wet
skin or sleep, but slowly crept
muttering to himself not yet not yet.

*

I was next a woman
and what happens once will happen all over again,
flitting out through the wetleaf ditches,
chuckling and snuffling.

Not all woman, not unfurred,
if she could sleep she might wake,
creeping under the neighbours' windows, rustling
    and whistling,
what happens once will happen all over again.

One night she began, like a ferret
slips out from the two-chambered holt of the heart,
she began to emerge. More and more
definite delicate lithe inarticulate

into the arms of her lover when
what happens once will happen all over again.
A frog
hopped under her red-alert eyes: She pounced.

*   *Frog*

Who's there? I am.
Where from? The wetlands of the womb.
First green, then lame,
going in and out of the swing door of the body.

Then secretive
lachrymal
vitreous
gelatinous.

I peeped out and saw myself
sitting like a stone in the rain
resting between forms.
This, I surmised,

with its throatful of grudges,
with its lumbar and glandular gripes, its guts,
its tissues and issues and sinews,
this is frog. For the moment.

This is when the sun
feels into my rubbery-soft-already-swumaway flesh
and finds me still
wedged in my inner dark.

So I croaked and carked,
clothed in leather in the bubbling breeding pools,
grieving being born and grown
and rotted down and born

    *

Ass

till I became a large-headed ash-coloured man
with long slouching ears,
living all alone in his hairy homespun body,
shitting and itching and scratching and eating;

who heard the crickets at twilight
amorously soliciting their wives all of willow-wand
    slimness,
little hieroglyphs in the grasses,
lifting their pale triangular heads.

Always describing and then discarding their
    throwaway world
and then leaping and listening to the tiny slippage
between real and technical time, I heard them
persistently telephoning and glorying in their
    lightness

saying 'Singing is who we are in this place.
We are made of digital sounds, we are seeking
to be slightly more precise than is possible,
whizzing around, trying to unconceal things
    literally momentary.'

From that day, I resolved to eat nothing but dew.
And did so and died, despite
my own huge eyes
that stared at me from behind.

*   *Sheep*

Crashed over backwards buried under all the layers
    of my body,
in this condition of contradictions
when the earth calls back her employee
from its long and regular work of falling and
    sleeping,

I lay in my last self, stricken, like a sheep on its back.
When up comes the jackel-headed god, the guide
    who herds the dead
and sniffed and frisked and found me already half
    rotted
in a little pile of teeth and broken bone laths

And said he could spare me in exchange for three
    truths.
Then first, I said, I don't want to see you again.
Second, I want you to go blind.
Third, I wish you and your kind would come to
    some violent end.

And off he went,
chasing some other scent,
muttering to himself
not yet not yet . . .

Three Portraits of a Radio Audience

JOHN LYNUM

Will you tune in now and listen to the voice of John Lynum,
Who drifts all night between hysteria and boredom.
Can't sleep, can't not sleep. A coin stuck in a slot,
Shapeless he lies. His voice is all he's got.
My god it's him alright, with his head under the blankets.
Cars and street-shouts are his come-and-go comforts.
He works nights you see – his job is wakefulness,
Twitching a half-kissed woman into focus.
Fair and new-fondled, frail and afraid to enter,
In the green interior of his eyes he sees her
Pause at his door and his whole bedroom shines
And flickers because she works with screens.
But it's ridiculous, he switches the light on.
And she has wings, though not yet open.

THE SONG AND DANCE MAN

Oh the poor tired rain, still dripping.
A very wet man walks, not quite not skipping.
Sings to himself, determined to preserve his
Sense of gaiety in spite of circumstances.
A little footshuffle. What does he know,
Does he know introspection and despair like us? Not so.
Wrapping the glow of his smile in the shreds of a rhythm,
The only light in this whole song-damaged region.
He knows a ballad yes but. Can he sing
Instruments of torture, that kind of thing?
Like apparently they make a slither in your abdomen
And pull your heart out here. If you're too human.

He doesn't know that no. that must be why
He's got red shoes on and a preposterous tie.

RACHEL RAYNOR

Who is Rachel. What is she. Not she.
Not what she says she is. Not her expression
Of routine touchiness. Not what you see,
Not the substantial substance of a woman.
Not her opponent eyes, not her concealed
And self-deceiving voices, not her heart's
Trampled-on dampness, not its four-inch field
Of nerves and shadows and night-wandering thoughts.
Not her incomparable soul, not its unique
Fidelity to failure, not the churr
Of its thin birdthroat, struggling to speak
On the bare perches of what stands for her.
Nor any name that anyone might try
To catch her with. As either she or I.

Another Westminster Bridge

go and glimpse the lovely inattentive water
discarding the gaze of many a bored street walker

where the weather trespasses into strip-lit offices
through tiny windows into tiny thoughts and authorities

and the soft beseeching tapping of typewriters

take hold of a breath-width instant, stare
at water which is already elsewhere
in a scrapwork of flashes and glittery flutters
and regular waves of apparently motionless motion

under the teetering structures of administration

where a million shut-away eyes glance once
restlessly at the river's ruts and glints

count five, then wander swiftly
away over the stone wing-bone of the city

Hymn to Iris

Quick-moving goddess of the rainbow
You whose being is only an afterglow of a passing-through

Put your hands
Put your heaven-taken shape down
On the ground. Now. Anywhere

Like a bent-down bough of nothing
A bridge built out of the linked cells of thin air

And let there be instantly in its underlight–
At street corners, on swings, out of car windows–
A three-moment blessing for all bridges

May impossible rifts be often delicately crossed
By bridges of two thrown ropes or one dropped plank

May the unfixed forms of water be warily leaned over
On flexible high bridges, huge iron sketches of the mathematics of
    strain
And bridges of see-through stone, the living-space of drips and
    echoes

May two fields be bridged by a stile
And two hearts by the tilting footbridge of a glance

And may I often wake on the broken bridge of a word,
Like in the wind the trace of a web. Tethered to nothing

Psalm to Sing in a Canoe

evening river that scarcely are
                        and us four in a plywood canoe

semi-resilient softness whose flatness is a floor for the barefoot
   steps of branches

were there not several windows where the water was clearly
   unfinished, I remember the unpaid stones looking up o black
   slat river, similar in size and scale to the strings of a cello

may your tum-ti-ti-tum bear our canoe into its vision at the misty

o geometrical straightness among billowings,
make good our partial emergence,

may we stay out long enough to lay our oars on our knees and
   still slide on in the rush with which clouds are swished together

may we come to the exact place and say so instantly, among a
   flash of flowers and the green shell song trees etcetera

o larval heaven, o finite quantity of freedom

in this marbled predicament, brought on by constantly alternating
   between stickles and pools
you whose beauty is only approximately its long and wishing
   reach,

may we come to know that the length of water is not quite the
   same as the passing of time,

may we make do with one glimpse each,
one eye one arm one bone
in our plywood canoe

River

in the black gland of the earth
the tiny inkling of a river

put your ear to the river you hear trees
put your ear to the trees you hear the widening
numerical workings of the river

right down the length of Devon,
under a milky square of light that keeps quite still

the river slows down and goes on

with storm trash clustered on its branches
and paper unfolding underwater
and pairs of ducks swimming over bright grass among flooded
    willows

the earth's eye
looking through the earth's bones

carries the moon carries the sun but keeps nothing

Tree Ghosts

a ballad with footnotes
(in which each letter commemorates a cut-down tree)

with thanks to Bram and Mary Bartlett and Clifford Harris

This is a b**A**llad for Clifford Harris
Who saw the last red squirrel on this estate.
A man of four long rods that slot together
Bending and trembling under a considerable topweight.

There was Jimmy Miller and Jack James, **B**rilliant axemen,
Bob Penn, a queen's scout, up a tree like a monkey,
Stan Ivy on transport. John Fulcher admin.
And this is **C**lifford Harris, the Last Red Squirrel man.

Whyoo whyoo whyoo, that's him making crosscuts
With bowsaws and pitsaws, I don't know how many years;
Anyone can slice **D**own but it requires a bit of accuracy
To get it all to fall like so, oak trees especially.

Put Clifford Harris on a great big mother oak
With l**E**gs **F**linging out and all sorts of bulges,
He could bring her down as neat as my arms
While a red squirrel nips in and watches.

Mind you he was employed to catch **G**reys,
Two shillings a tail. He got all sorts of **H**atred
But when it's your work you've got to get on with it.
He had long squirrel rods for poking the dreys.

Alum**I**nium things, they wouldn't go up straight,
Which was one of the hardest jobs for your arms;
And plus you've got to go out when it's wet
And the rain runs rivers up the sleeves of your **J**acket.

Well this is a ballad about those times,
Almost always there, you don't taKe a lot of notice,
When the red was still at large in the woods,
So tame you could talk to him, says Clifford Harris.

He says the red was a gentle littLe thing
Who'd hop up with tail back looking down on you motionless,
Always very busy at providing for the winter,
Whereas your grey is shy and not nearly so clever.

So I ask you to picture hiM walking by earsight
Down the rides at North Woods, with his rods and lunchpack
Through blocks of chiffchaffs singing in the broadleaves
And the odd nuthatch in the fissures of conifers.

Next thing he knows, there's a terrific Noise.
Yes sometimes it does sound weird in a wood,
Sometimes it's like the wind's on all fours
Bleeding to death and you never say a word;

Certain places where there's nothing but nettles
And wonderful ash trees and a glimpse of a rOe deer,
If you stop rustling about you can hear
Whatever the wind says when there's no one there.

Well Clifford he Peers round and he sees three greys
Attacking a red. The red's all panicky
And clicking at Clifford as if saying 'help me!'
It's as if that sQuirrel was one of his family.

But what could he do? You can't step in.
It's the same as trees. Once they start to go
It cReaks and cracks and nothing can stop them.
WhooSh! Gone! It's like holding snow.

It's like the fuTure's got a certain momentum,
It's like Tony Webster rolled down the log load,
One minute up, Unroping the stanchions,
Next minute crippled to the end of his days.

And that was the Very last red squirrel.
Since then it's been nothing but greys.
It's like the Woodlark it's like many a one
That you take for granted; neXt thing it's gone.

It's like sheering wood from the small end up,
You're turning the lathe and layer by laYer,
WhizzZ! Something you'd never think would happen.
The tree's ghost floats into the air!

FOOTNOTES

A is for Ash Trees
the loftiest letters in the wooden alphabet
B is for Beech Trees and Birch Trees
made of many streaming blooming intucking unfurling
C is for both Copse and Corpse
as G is for both Grove and Grave
in which you sow a person
and he puts forth silvery threads into the air
and AIR is for the varying shapes
made by the cavities of the mouth and throat
so that the soul is squeezed and shaken into VOICE

    *

D E F is the Deaf and Dumb and Finger language of the branches
L M N is thousands of leaf-like sounds
that shadow forth for a moment in the wake of wind
like a rock or stick inscribes its drift in the scrolls of a river
I, by far the most solitary and inward-looking letter,

I is for Speech Impediment
in which the timber's stutter doesn't interest the woodman
and Hyale Crocale Phiale Meliae – these are for Dryads and Hamadryads,
their bodies tushed to one side to be slatted and planked up
whereas J and K are for Joists and Krucks
made of a Woodnymph's Joints and Kracks

*

O is the Outline of the OldWood
and S is the Still Growing Ghost of the OldWood
in which the waters recompose as the vapour-forms of twigs and anti-
    twigs, roots and un-roots
and P and Q are Songs of eQuivocal Perplexity
issuing from the throats of Oaks
and T is for the Shakes which is when Timber if you cut it Green
it splits in a hot summer
plus you've got V which is like the funny bone of a conifer
and if you Bang it you get pins and needles
not to mention W which is a Woodlark
which is what emerges when the Larches drop their Aitches

*

but R is for Rowan, the Quicken Tree,
which is even now breathlessly quickening into wings tails crests
threads flames flumes fans palms scarves robes tubes
and perpetually interchangeable billows following one after another
and U is for the Unreadable Alphabet of its Leaves
each one a single phase out of the sequence of movements in the flight of
    birds
and X and Z are for the criss-crossed Zones
of the living and the dead wood
in which Y is for Yew, which grows by graves
and is said to spread a root like a kind of windpipe
to the mouth of every corpse

A Star Here And A Star There

the first whisper of stars is a faint thing
a candle sound, too far away to read by

the first whisper of stars is a candle sound
those faraway stars that rise and give themselves airs
      a star here and a star there
the first whisper of stars is that faint thing
that candle sound too far away to read by

when you walk outside leaving the door ajar
and smell the various Danks of Dusk
      and a star here
      and a star there

you walk outside leaving the door ajar
and one by one those stars bring you their troubles
      and a star
those deafmute stars – Alkaid Mizar Alioth –
trying to make you hear who they once were
      and a star
      here and there
      and
      here and there the
      start of a
Phad Merak Muscida – it's like blowing on a ring of cinders
all that sky that lies hidden in the taken for granted air

it's like blowing on a ring of cinders
the crackle of not quite stars that you can hear
when you walk outside leaving the door ajar
and smell the various Danks of Dusk

and here and there
the start
of a star

someone looks up, he sees his soul growing visible
in various shapes above the house

he sees his soul tilted above the house
all his opponent selves hanging and fluttering
out there in the taken for granted air
in various shapes above the house
                star
he sees a star here and a star there
and a star here
and a star a star
here and there he sees

there flies that man they call the moon,
that bone-thin man, his body almost gone
                star
there he flies among the stars,
that deafmute man, urgently making signs
among those first faint stars
those whispered stars, their meanings almost gone

Moon Hymn

I will give you one glimpse
a glimpse of the moon's grievance
whose appearance is all pocks and points
that look like frost-glints

I will wave my hand to her
in her first quarter
when the whole world is against her
shadowy exposure of her centre

o the moon loves to wander
I will go clockwise and stare
when she is huge when she is half elsewhere
half naked, in struggle with the air

and growing rounder and rounder
a pert peering creature
I love her sidling and awkward
when she's not quite circular

o criminal and ingrown
skinned animal o moon
carrying inside yourself your own
death's head, your dark one

why do you chop yourself away
piece by piece, to that final trace
of an outline of ice
on a cupful of space?

The mud-spattered recollections of a woman who lived her life backwards

I'll tell you a tale: one morning one morning I lay
in my uncomfortable six-foot small grave,
I lay sulking about a somewhat too short-lit
life both fruitful and dutiful.

It was death it was death like an inbreath fully inhaled
in the grief of the world when at last
there began to emerge a way out, alas
the in-snowing silence made any description difficult.

No eyes no matches and yet mathematically speaking
I could still reach at a stretch a wispish whiteish
last seen outline any way up, which could well be my own
were it only a matter of re-folding.

So I creased I uncreased and the next thing I knew
I was pulled from the ground at the appointed hour
and rushed to the nearest morgue to set out yet again
from the bed to the floor to the door to the air.

And there was the car still there in its last known place
under the rain where I'd left it, my husband etc.
even myself, in retrospect I was still there
still driving back with the past all spread out already in front of
  me.

What a refreshing whiff with the windows open!
there were the dead leaves twitching and tacking back

to their roosts in the trees and all it required
was a certain minimum level of inattention.

I tell you, for many years from doorway to doorway
and in through a series of rooms I barely noticed
I was humming the same tune twice, I was seeing the same
three children racing towards me getting smaller and smaller.

This tale's like a rose, once opened it
cannot reclose, it continues: one morning
one terrible morning for maybe the hundredth time
they came to insert my third child back inside me.

It was death it was death: from head to foot
I heard myself crack with the effort, I leaned and cried
and a feeling fell on me with a dull clang
that I'd never see my darling daughter again.

Then both my sons, slowly at first
then faster and faster, their limbs retracted inwards
smaller and smaller till all that remained
was a little mound where I didn't quite meet in the middle.

Well either I was or was not either living or dead
in a windowless cubicle of the past, a mere
8.3 light minutes from the present moment when at last
my husband walked oh dear he walked me to church.

All in one brief winter's day, both
braced for confusion with much shy joy,
reversed our vows, unringed our hands
and slid them back in our pockets God knows why.

What then what then I'll tell you what then: one evening
there I stood in the matchbox world of childhood
and saw the stars fall straight through Jimmy's binoculars,
they looked so weird skewered to a fleeting instant.

Then again and again for maybe the hundredth time
they came to insert me feet first back into nothing
complete with all my missing hopes – next morning
there was that same old humming thrum still there.

That same old humming thrumming sound that is either
my tape re-winding again or maybe it's stars
passing through stars coming back to their last known places,
for as far as I know in the end both sounds are the same.

Various Portents

Various stars. Various kings.
Various sunsets, signs, cursory insights.
Many minute attentions, many knowledgeable watchers,
Much cold, much overbearing darkness.

Various long midwinter Glooms.
Various Solitary and Terrible Stars.
Many Frosty Nights, many previously Unseen
    Sky-flowers.
Many people setting out (some of them kings) all clutching at
    stars.

More than one North Star, more than one South Star.
Several billion elliptical galaxies, bubble nebulae, binary systems,
Various dust lanes, various routes through varying thicknesses of
    Dark,
Many tunnels into deep space, minds going back and forth.

Many visions, many digitally enhanced heavens,
All kinds of glistenings being gathered into telescopes:
Fireworks, gasworks, white-streaked works of Dusk,
Works of wonder and/or water, snowflakes, stars of frost . . .

Various dazed astronomers dilating their eyes,
Various astronauts setting out into laughterless earthlessness,
Various 5,000-year-old moon maps,
Various blindmen feeling across the heavens in braille.

Various gods making beautiful works in bronze,
Brooches, crowns, triangles, cups and chains,
And all sorts of drystone stars put together without mortar.
Many Wisemen remarking the irregular weather.

Many exile energies, many low-voiced followers,
Watchers of wisps of various glowing spindles,
Soothsayers, hunters in the High Country of the Zodiac,
Seafarers tossing, tied to a star . . .

Various people coming home (some of them kings). Various
    headlights.
Two or three children standing or sitting on the low wall.
Various winds, the Sea Wind, the sound-laden Winds of Evening
Blowing the stars towards them, bringing snow.

Excursion to the Planet Mercury

certain evenings a little before the golden
foam of the horizon has properly hardened
you can see a tiny iron island
very close indeed to the sun.

all craters and mirrors, the uncanny country
of the planet Mercury – a mystery
without I without air,
without you without sound.

in that violently magic little place
the sky is racing along
like a blue wrapper flapped and let go
from a car window.

now hot now cold
the ground moves fast,
a few stones frisk about
looking for a foothold

but it shales it slides
the whole concept is only
loosely fastened
to a few weak tweaks of gravity.

o the weather is dreadful there:
thousand-year showers of dust
all dandruff and discarded shells
of creatures too swift to exist:

paupers beggars toughs
boys in dresses
who come alive and crumble
at the mercy of metamorphosis.

no nothing accumulates there
not even mist
nothing but glimmering beginnings
making ready to manifest.

as for the catastrophe
of nights on mercury,
hiding in a rock-smashed hollow
at about two hundred degrees below zero

the feather-footed winds
take off their guises there,
they go in gym shoes
thieving and lifting

and their amazed expressions
have been soundproofed, nevertheless
they go on howling
for gladness sheer gladness

Sonnet

Spacecraft Voyager 1 has boldly gone
into Deep Silence carrying a gold-plated disc inscribed with
    whale-song
it has bleeped back a last infra-red fragment of language
and floated way way up over the jagged edge
of this almost endless bright and blowy enclosure of weather
to sink through a new texture as tenuous as the soft upward
    pressure of an elevator
and go on and on falling up steep flights of blackness with
    increasing swiftness
beyond the Crystalline Cloud of the Dead beyond Plato beyond
    Copernicus
O meticulous swivel cameras still registering events
among those homeless spaces gathering in that silence
that hasn't yet had time to speak   in that increasing sphere
of tiny runaway stars notched in the year
now you can look closely at massless light
that is said to travel freely but is probably in full flight